Talking Hands
FOOD

COMIDA

Published in the United States of America by The Child's World®
PO Box 326, Chanhassen, MN 55317-0326
800-599-READ
www.childsworld.com

Photo Credits: Digital Stock: 18; Photodisc/Burke/Triolo Productions: cover (left and right), 1 (left and right), 2, 3, 4, 5, 6, 7, 9, 10, 11, 12, 13, 14, 15, 16, 17, 19, 20, 21, 22, 23; Stockbyte: 8.

The Child's World®: Mary Berendes, Publishing Director

Editorial Directions, Inc.: E. Russell Primm, Editorial Director; Katie Marsico and Elizabeth K. Martin, Associate Editors; Kathleen Petelinsek and E. Russell Primm, Photo Researchers

The Design Lab: Kathleen Petelinsek, design, and page production

LIBRARY OF CONGRESS CATALOGING-IN-PUBLICATION DATA
Petelinsek, Kathleen.
  Food = Comida / by Kathleen Petelinsek and E. Russell Primm III ; content advisers, Carmine L. Vozzolo and Kim Bianco Majeri.
     p. cm. — (Talking hands)
  Summary: Provides illustrations of American Sign Language signs and Spanish and English text for various foods.
  English, Spanish, and American Sign Language.
  ISBN 1-59296-020-0 (lib. bdg. : alk. paper) 1. American Sign Language—Vocabulary—Juvenile literature. 2. Spanish language—Vocabulary—Juvenile literature. 3. Food—Juvenile literature. [1. American Sign Language—Vocabulary. 2. Spanish language—Vocabulary. 3. Polyglot materials. 4. Food.] I. Title: Comida II. Primm, E. Russell, 1958– III. Title.
  HV2476.P475 2004
  419'.7—dc22
                                                2003018693

NOTE TO PARENTS AND EDUCATORS:
The understanding of any language begins with the acquisition of vocabulary, whether the language is spoken or manual. The books in the Talking Hands series provide readers, both young and old, with a first introduction to basic American Sign Language signs. Combining close photo cues and simple, but detailed, line illustration, children and adults alike can begin the process of learning American Sign Language. In addition to the English word and sign for that word, we have included the Spanish word. The addition of the Spanish word is a wonderful way to allow children to see multiple ways (English, Spanish, signed) to say the same word. This is also beneficial for Spanish-speaking families to learn the sign even though they may not know the English word for that object.

Let these books be an introduction to the world of American Sign Language. Most languages have regional dialects and multiple ways of expressing the same thought. This is also true for sign language. We have attempted to use the most common version of the signs for the words in this series. As with any language, the best way to learn is to be taught in person by a frequent user. It is our hope that this series will pique your interest in sign language.

Apple
Manzana

1.

Repeat
Repita

Banana
Plátano

1.

2.

Motion peeling a banana.
Haga el gesto de pelar
un plátano.

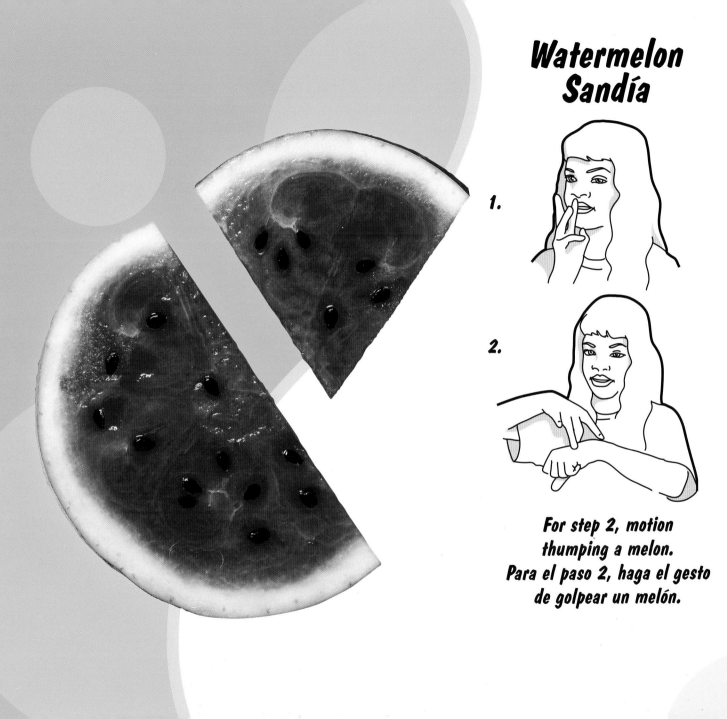

Watermelon
Sandía

1.

2.

**For step 2, motion thumping a melon.
Para el paso 2, haga el gesto de golpear un melón.**

Orange
Naranja

1.

2.

Repeat
Repita

Strawberry
Fresa

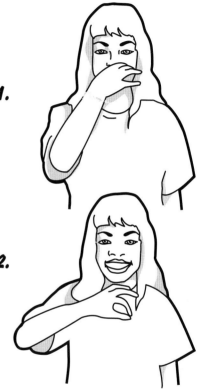

1.

2.

Tomato
Tomate

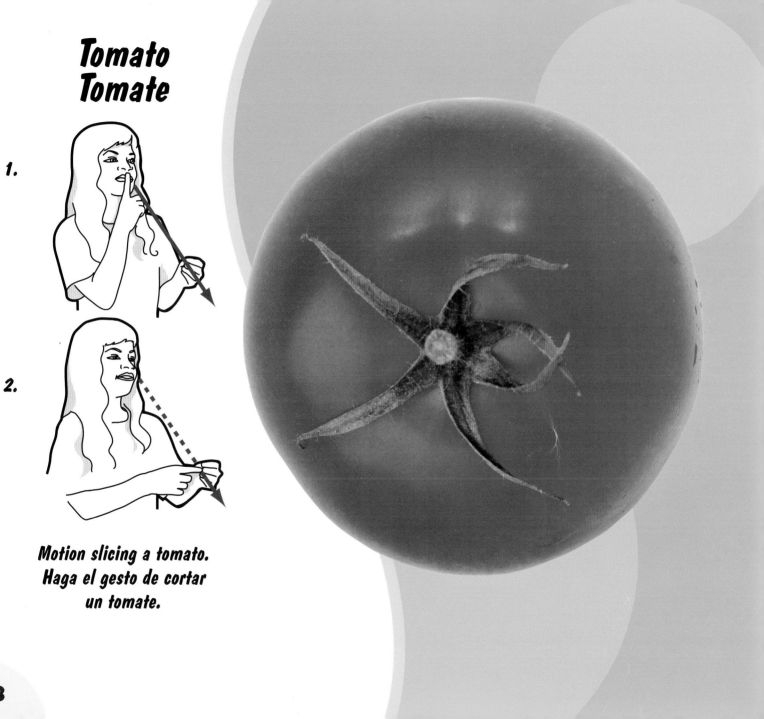

1.

2.

Motion slicing a tomato.
Haga el gesto de cortar
un tomate.

Corn
Maíz

1.

2.

Motion eating a cob of corn,
twisting and moving the
cob right to left.
Haga el gesto de comer una
mazorca de maíz, torciendo y
moviendo la mazorca de
derecha a izquierda.

9

Hamburger
Hamburguesa

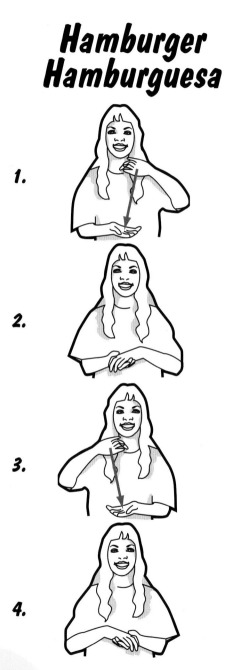

1.

2.

3.

4.

10

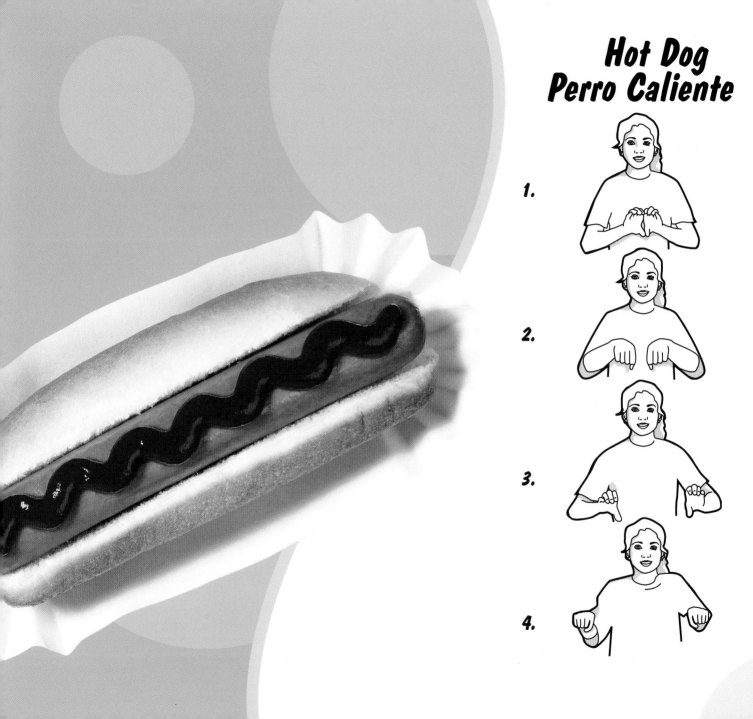

Hot Dog
Perro Caliente

1.

2.

3.

4.

Chicken
Pollo

1.

2.

Repeat
Repita

Egg
Huevo

1.

2.

13

Fish
Pescado

1.

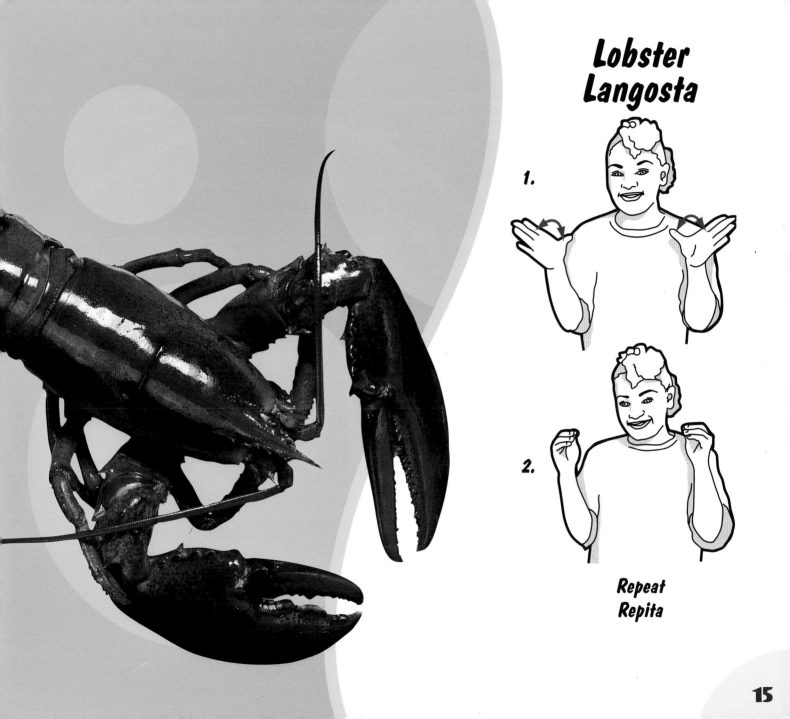

Lobster
Langosta

1.

2.

Repeat
Repita

15

Soup
Sopa

1.

2.

Repeat
Repita

Bread
Pan

1.

Motion slicing bread.
Haga el gesto de
cortar el pan.

Coffee
Café

1.

Milk
Leche

1.

2.

Repeat
Repita

19

Pie
Tarta

1.

2.

Ice Cream
Helado

1.

2.

Repeat
Repita

Chocolate
Chocolate

1.

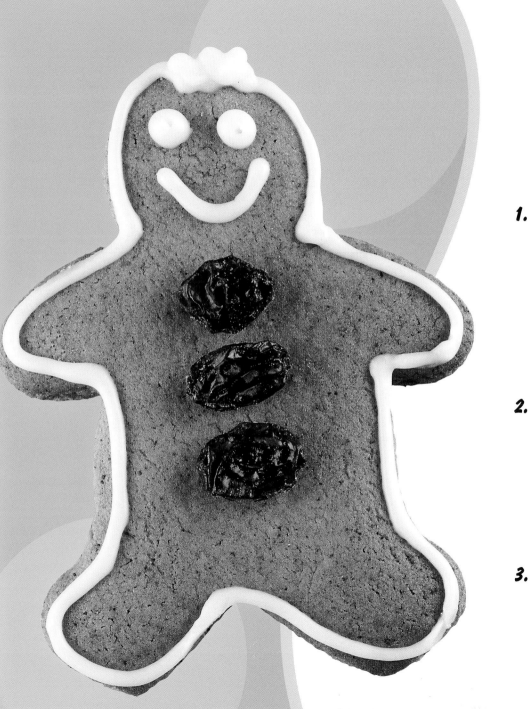

Cookie
Galleta

1.

2.

3.

23

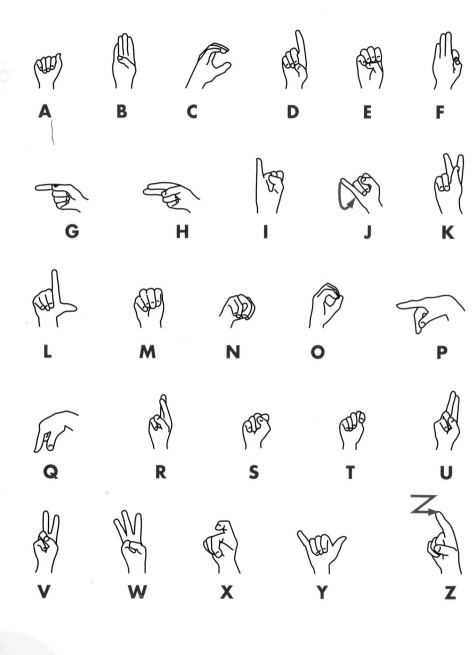

A B C D E F

G H I J K

L M N O P

Q R S T U

V W X Y Z

A SPECIAL THANK-YOU

to our models from the Program for Children Who Are Deaf and Hard of Hearing at the Alexander Graham Bell Elementary School in Chicago, Illinois:

Aroosa is in third grade in Milwaukee and loves reading, shopping, and playing with her sister Aamna. Aroosa's favorite color is red.

Carla is in fourth grade and enjoys art, as well as all kinds of sports.

Deandre likes playing football and watching NFL games on television. He also looks forward to going to the movies with his family.

Destiny enjoys music and dancing. She especially likes learning new things and spends much of her time practicing her cursive handwriting.

Xiomara loves fashion, clothes, and jewelry. She also enjoys music and dancing. Xiomara's favorite animal is the cat.

24